the good
the bad
the unforgettable

Published by Anchor Print Group Limited

April 2013

Compiled by Vicki Smith
on behalf of Leicestershire Teenage Pregnancy Partnership

Compilation © Leicestershire Teenage Pregnancy Partnership 2013

Contributions © individual copyright holders

ISBN: 978-1-907540-84-4

To get in touch email tellmemore@parentsunder20.co.uk

The Good, The Bad, The Unforgettable is a collection of letters, thoughts and memories from people who are, or were, young parents.

We have created this book to share our experiences – joyful and difficult – of being a young parent. We wanted to offer other young parents and their families reassurance, hope and the realisation that they are not alone.

The book contains details of personal experiences and situations, not always pleasant – however we wanted to share them without using rose tinted glasses.

"Being a young parent seems to make some people think your life is free for open discussion and they can make rude comments about you and it won't hurt you. To anyone who thinks that I'd like to tell you it does hurt more than you could ever understand."

It would be nice if people would praise and support us instead of doubting us because you might make us doubt ourselves.

You can't judge a person until you've walked a mile in their shoes.

Leicestershire County Young Parents Forum xx

Dear Society,

Eighteen and pregnant, my life had ended. How would I become the successful person I hoped to be when I had ended up in this shameful state? I might as well give up now. I would not be able to achieve everything I had hoped for, everything I had dreamed of. That is it. Eighteen. Pregnant. The end. Society, that is what you said.

Society, you were cruel. At a time when I felt most vulnerable and needed every ounce of confidence, you served to shoot me down. Directly, and indirectly, you made me feel like a worthless parasite, the scourge of our modern Britain. Even family and friends, who I dearly loved, felt that it was the end for me, because Society, that is the impact you have. You control thoughts and you control perceptions. My so called 'feckless' behaviour had a consequence that had apparently led to the end of my life. I just had to get on and deal with it.

Although unplanned, I chose to keep my baby, a decision that was right for me. A decision that I am proud of. I could have bowed to pressure and I knew what people thought, but they weren't me. They hadn't started to develop that little gut feeling. A little sensation of determination that was smouldering away and a sense that, actually, things would be ok.

I will admit Society, pregnancy was not great. As soon as the first three months of relentless tiredness and nausea were over, my 'predicament' started to become visible and I had you to contend with. I dropped out of college, just as you expected me to. I had to claim benefits, just like you said. After all, who would want to employ an irresponsible teenager? I could cope with all this to some extent. It was the looks and the judgement that was the most difficult. This affected me in a way I shall never forget.

Complete strangers took it upon themselves to judge me in one glance. To sum up in a millisecond that I was that bad of a person, I was worthy of a dirty look from a person I did not know. Those looks, surprisingly enough, had the desired effect of making me feel dirty and shameful.

Why Society? Why would you inflict such contempt on a young girl who happened to be pregnant, and happened to want to do her best?

I was lucky enough to be able to live with my mother until I was twenty-one. I know this will shock you Society because I often hear you saying that the only reason I put myself through the judgment is for a council house. I often wonder if you've ever seen a council house, they are not the most desirable of properties. Do you not think I hope for more? There was only ever one reason that I put myself through your judgment Society, and that was my light of the end of my nine month long tunnel.

My baby, my boy, my beautiful, sweet, innocent child. Born free from your influence, free from your burden, but unfortunately not free from your judgment. According to you there was only one road for him, the child of a teenage parent. Let us not forget Society, you know it all.

Through all your judgment Society, one thing had been constantly fuelled. That smouldering feeling of determination had snowballed into a blazing fire that wanted to shield my innocent little boy from your damage. I wanted to stick my middle finger up at you Society because who the hell did you think you were to judge me?

My confidence had been shattered but I was ready to fight back. I telephoned college for a place back on my A Levels. I expected to be greeted with open arms, with people pleased that I wasn't sitting on my backside claiming benefits, like you keep telling them Society. I was wrong. I will hold my hands up Society, I underestimated you. I was told quite frankly, no. I would not be able to cope with the workload because I was a teenage parent. What I could not understand Society, was why you had told people that? How did you know what I could and could not do?

Luckily this only extinguished some of the flames and I enrolled on a part-time course in Health and Social Care. This was not what I wanted to do at all but it was a more sensible option considering my limits, right Society?

I put in the work, achieved highly in all of my modules and gained some confidence. I was pleased Society, but I was far from satisfied. This taste of learning had merely whetted my appetite and fuelled my fire. Was this really all I could do Society? You kept telling me it was and that I was 'lucky' that I had achieved what I had on that course. I was happy, but I wanted more, a lot more. Why shouldn't I try? My boy deserves it, I deserve it.

I applied for two Access to Higher Education courses. One in law and then one in social sciences in case I did not get my first choice. There was no way I would be allowed to study on the law course I thought, but what did I have to lose? Much to my surprise, and probably yours too Society, I was invited to an interview and offered a place on the course.

That was it, that was the boost I needed. I was going to do well and provide for my precious little boy. I worked even harder that following year and again I achieved high marks in all my modules. My confidence blossomed and so did my drive, but do not worry Society, I was not getting ahead of myself. You were always lurking around to keep me in my place.

I shall never forget the time I was at the bus stop with a friend on my way home from college. I had been given a distinction in an assignment and was giggly and excited. Two young men were behind us in the queue. One questioned our celebratory chit chat and my friend explained. I said I was really pleased and looking forward to getting home to my son to give him a big cuddle. "You have a baby?" Yes, I replied. "Slag". It felt like I had been shot with a bullet full of shame. I froze and felt it spread throughout every inch of my body. That Society, felt brutal.

Not long afterwards I had been on my way home on the bus with my son. He was all snug and happy in his pushchair with his rosy cheeks beaming away. There was an old couple sat at the front of the bus talking very loudly and in tones of disgust. It did not take me long to realise it was me and my son they were talking about Society. My little innocent boy. "They go out and get pregnant so they can claim benefits and get a house. It's a disgrace, never happened in my day". I will be honest Society, this time you really got the better of me and I was angry. Unfortunately the old couple got off the bus at the same stop as me. I marched up to them and blurted out "how dare you judge me, it is people like you that give old people a bad name". It was not my finest moment Society but I was hurt and upset. Looking back I can see that my behaviour only led to further judgment – a young girl with a pram giving an old couple a piece of her mind on a busy street. I was certainly fitting your mould then Society.

Still, I was undeterred and my fire was growing with everything you threw at me. That year I earned myself a place on a law degree at a red brick university. Finally, finally Society I was proving you wrong. On the outside at least. On the inside I was not convinced. I had moved into a two bedroomed house and was struggling with the adjustment. My workload had increased massively and I had to learn how to balance running a home, be a good mother and work for a law degree. I started to worry Society. I thought you may be right. I thought I couldn't cope. People like me could not achieve things like this. My little boy kept me going.

I stopped worrying about having a perfectly tidy house. It became very disorganised, but it was clean. My boy was my priority and that meant working hard to give him a bright future. The house could wait. It was a stepping stone anyway. We were not going to be here for the long term, although I am sure that is what you expected Society.

Although I got some help with paying my rent, I struggled at first with my student loan. I took a year out after the first year of my degree and worked full time to build up some savings. This year was a welcomed break from study. I reflected upon my first year at university and went back into my second year even more determined to succeed.

I used to wonder what you thought of me at this point Society but I think I knew deep down. I was reminded by the look on people's faces when I said I was a mother, particularly at university. Some people were even shocked I was there – according to you Society, people like me did not go to university, did we? We sat living a life of luxury that only benefits could provide, in the council houses we had always longed for. I ended up keeping myself to myself. I was there for one reason and I was going to get what I wanted.
After years of blood, sweat and plenty of tears, I gained my law degree – LLB (hons) Law 2:1. That was it, I had done it, I had showed you Society, or had I?

It did not take me long to realise Society that I may never show you. I may never change your mind. You will always judge and always hurt, because Society you are cruel when you want to be. The only thing I can do Society, is to stop caring what you think and to pity you because you will never change. My story and all the others like it are kept hidden because god help you if people knew the truth. God help you if people knew about all the teenage mothers out there that have become lawyers, teachers, nurses, accountants, doctors, writers and so on. God help society if people did not actually think becoming a teenage parent led to a life on benefits.

Society I was a teenage parent, I relied on benefits when I needed to and I lived on a housing estate. I am a lecturer, I have a Masters degree, I own my own home, I drive my own car, and I pay tax. Most importantly, I provide for my son who is happy and healthy and thriving. I am proud of each and every aspect of who I am and what I have achieved, do you hear that Society? I AM PROUD.

The one thing I do hope Society, is that you change your message. I hope that you do not hold other teenage parents back and I hope that they do not believe you when you tell them that they cannot achieve their dreams. I hope you encourage and empower young parents. I hope they can live their lives happily and free from judgment. If that fails Society, I hope they find the strength inside themselves to stick their middle finger up at you as I have done.

Forever hopeful,

Sarah Kennedy

My name is Jessica, I am twenty years old and I have a one year old son..... I wonder what your first impressions are of me? Well whatever you're thinking I'm sure I've heard it before! Being a young parent seems to make some people think your life is free for open discussion and they can make rude comments about you and it won't hurt you. To anyone who thinks that I'd like to tell you it does hurt more that you could ever understand. I would never have imagined that we would have our own little house, jobs well paid enough to afford it and our own little family two years ago.

Here is my story:

At 18 I had taken my qualifications, I had a job, me and my partner had been together for 4 years. I enjoyed spending money on make-up and nice things for myself but not that I knew it my whole world was about to be tipped upside down! I think deep down in my heart I knew I was pregnant, I just didn't want to admit it. I was pretending nothing felt different but Jason knew something was wrong and told me to take a test. After a couple of days I gave in and took the test but the problem was I couldn't look. I passed it to him and I could see in his face what it said, he didn't need to tell me and that's the moment my life changed for the better.

During my pregnancy I had it all, the sideways looks from old ladies on the bus, the awkward faces when I told people I worked with I was pregnant, there was one man who shouted fat at me down the street – I WAS 8 MONTHS PREGNANT! Possibly the worst thing was someone who I used to go to school with throwing a sandwich at me from her car window.

How does anyone deserve that? But I would do all of that again 100 x for my son. The moment he was placed on my chest after two days of labour and an emergency c-section was the proudest moment of my life, during our time in hospital my partner was the first at the door to see his baby. He was in much in love as I was, our family was perfect.

Being a mum is hard at the best of times, there's so many things you don't factor in before you have a baby, how will I cope when they are ill, keeping on top of running a house with a child on your hip and carting round weeks worth of things every time you leave the house! But the good is so much better than the bad, when that naughty little boy looks up at me and laughs and says mama I can't be mad that he's just trashed the clean living room. In the middle of the night when he just won't sleep the moment he cuddles up to me and sighs my heart melts all over again. It may sound like a lot of work to some people that is because it is, but being a parent is the most inspiring job there is because you're never alone.

That little person loves you just as much as you love them. True, unconditional love no matter how old you are.

xxxx

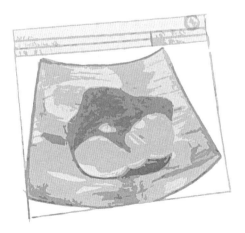

I was 18, young, free and enjoying life when I did the pregnancy test. It was negative so back in the pack it went! For some reason I didn't throw it away, just placed it on the side. A week went by and I was with my sister joking about being pregnant, I saw the negative test packet and re-opened it... then there it was staring me in the face.... 2 lines.... Pregnant?....

I was in shock, I ran up to my mum in bed but she was tired and thought I was being silly, my sister said they change but I knew!! I rang my friend and stayed the night, the next day I did 5 more tests before going to the doctors and demanding another. It was official, I was pregnant! I couldn't make any sense of my emotions but I knew this baby wasn't going anywhere, I had only just got back with my boyfriend of 2 years after a 4 month break. I needed to know how far pregnant I was!!

The first scan came and I knew the little smudge on the screen wasn't my boyfriend's. We spoke and he decided to stay. I was SO happy!!

Through the pregnancy people made rude comments and nasty comments. I just held my head high. My due date came and went. I was exhausted.... Excited and nervous! Then 5 days late the pains started. Before I could blink I was holding a beautiful baby boy. I knew from that moment this little life in front of me was also MY whole life too. I was amazed as we looked into each others eyes! Perfect!

The days, weeks, months went by so fast, being a mummy was stressful but so rewarding. The love I had for this amazing child was unbelievable! Me, my baby boy and partner were a happy family. Unfortunately my baby's real dad wasn't interested.... I just thought his loss!!! I got myself a house and made it a home even though it was expensive and lonely my little man brightened it up by learning every day and with that my love was growing with every new step he took. Words can't describe the feelings.

Now my not so little man is a year old in 2 days, how time flies. Unfortunately my partner left me and wants nothing more to do with us, that hurt me a lot to know he walked out on what I classed as his son. It's such a shame and I am now getting threats and being told I'm a bad mother! I know I'm not and who cares what people think! I have my little boy and he makes me so happy, it's an honour to be his mommy! I love him with all my heart and he loves me too…. He is all I need in life.

It's hard being a teenage mum but people can judge so quick… they don't understand and when they do, well good luck to them they will need it.

It's me and you doodle, forever and always! I love you

Kacie

xxxx

I met Chloe when she was 20 weeks pregnant. I was 20 and she was 17. We began seeing each other and this was the beginning of our relationship.

When I found out that Chloe was pregnant I was scared. Being in a relationship with someone who was pregnant with someone else's child did not bother me and we made plans to bring up the baby together and I was happy to take on the roles and responsibilities of being a father.

Telling my parents was a petrifying thought, so I just took Chloe round to the house and introduced her. My mum's reaction was shock & disappointment, as mum thought I could do better than Chloe. They did not think I would be committed and would run when the baby was born. My Dad seemed to be a lot more chilled and was fine with it.

Gradually my mum started to come round to the idea once she realised we were in a serious relationship.

The birth of our baby boy made me happy and I felt an instant attachment to him. He felt like my son and I wanted to care and protect him forever.

Being a dad was really scary and I had support from Sure Start to overcome some of my fears like bathing for the first time. I also attended a "Being Dad" programme to support me, which I found really good & interesting and it helped me a lot to understand my role in becoming a father.

Juggling a full time job and being a parent is hard work, but you can't change it and you have to get on with it. I still find time to spend quality time with my son and I attend Dad's sessions, where I get chance to meet other fathers.

I have recently found out that we are pregnant again. Although this child will be biologically mine it will make no difference to how I feel towards our first child.

By Chris (21)

I was 17 when I found out I was pregnant, my partner, Craig, was 23. we had been together 1 and a half years. Craig had found out before we met that there was a 3% chance of him fathering his own child. I was on the implant but came off it and didn't think we had to protect against anything, so we didn't!

We spoke about, for the future, adoption, IVF etc., that broke our hearts but life is a funny old game. I used to joke after sex and lay up against the wall & say 'I'm getting pregnant this time', guess what? it worked! ..

I was around 14 weeks when we found out after me being ill for a good few weeks. I was sent for an emergency scan as they thought I was having an ectopic pregnancy, all was well with the baby & he was growing fab! I was always in hospital, because my little tinker loved to not move for days! I was in so often they named a room after me!..

At 36 weeks, my worst nightmare, I haemorrhaged badly. The hospital sent an ambulance and I was kept in. I kept haemorrhaging, and they were worried that my placenta was coming away from the wall so after 3 days in hospital, they started me off (induced).

I gave birth to my beautiful but tiny 5lb 5oz baby boy, 4 weeks early. I haemorrhaged again after having him, so he got rushed to my partner. it was well into the night when we were on the ward that I got my first proper cuddle, he was so dinky & small, we were scared to hold him! He's now 8 months, and is thriving! He's way above his age and it's just amazing seeing him and how much he has grown!

Thank you for reading :)

Toni

Early last spring had anyone asked if I understood, had any real idea of what changes where to come, then my answer back would have been "of course, looking forward to it". Looking back, the truth is I had no idea, ask me today and my answer would simply be "no, I did not. I didn't have the faintest idea". Advice came at me from all angles, I heard the words, went through the motions, but did it register, did it sink in at all? Absolutely not. The worry, panic and difficult decisions of that spring, pale in comparison to what was to come. I'm not saying it was a bad thing, not for one minute, ignorance was bliss. I had great friends, a supportive family, it was all going to be fine.

It wasn't when I found out I was pregnant at fourteen that things changed, weirdly things remained the same. Sometimes I would momentarily forget about my predicament, then a glance down at my swelling belly brought it all back to the forefront of my consciousness again. But it was all good, I was happy. I shopped for baby clothes, got the crib ready, packed my hospital bag. I knew school was more important than ever now and I worked hard.

Baby Alfie was born at nine thirty two in the morning. It had been hard work, scary, terrifying in fact, but I'd done it. I'd come out the other side with a beautiful baby boy. I was tired and sore, but I'd done it. Messages of congratulations poured in, I couldn't have been happier.

I had expected, I suppose to be ripped apart physically, but I hadn't expected to be so emotionally torn. I couldn't have been more wrong. Physically I was in great shape, there's a lot to be said for having a baby so young, but I had an emotional rollercoaster ahead of me. Hair, make-up and facebook were no longer the centre of my universe, I had a new centre of gravity, worlds apart from the old one.

As I got to know my son, got into a routine, my life changed beyond recognition.

I don't blame them, how could they possibly understand what life is like for me, I don't believe any woman, whatever age knows what they're letting themselves in for when they embark on motherhood, so how could my friends know? It's not just the chores, the dressing, the feeding, the bottle making, the bathing, the singing nursery rhymes, the reading books, I can't really call those chores, its being emotionally torn that came as a surprise. I need my friends; I want to know what's going on at the weekend, who's seeing who, keep up with all the gossip. I want my old life, but I love my new life too. Trying to bring those two worlds together, that's a challenge.

I don't think I'll ever find the answer to that one. My friends simply won't understand until they become mothers themselves, and that could be a long time coming. My friends have a different centre of gravity to me, we do have some things in common, but our priorities are different and that's the crux of the problem. Hanging out, drinking, partying, that's not me anymore. If given the chance to go back to my old way of life, I'm not sure at all I would take it. Hair, make-up, facebook, there's more to life.

Before I became a mother I now realise I was selfish, not selfish in a negative way but selfish because I literally only had myself to worry about. I couldn't have known how much I could care for another human being, care for their physical needs and care for them and love them until I could burst, care for someone so much I would literally die for them. I knew the moment my baby arrived that he was number one, if it came to it, I would take a bullet for him, I hadn't known my own capacity for love.

In a years time, in five years time, in ten years time, I wonder how my life will have changed again, the up the downs, the highs and the lows. I want a good job, a nice home; I'm prepared to work for it. Maybe I'm being naive, maybe I'll look back and say change took me by surprise again. For now I think I've seen enough change for a fifteen year old, more change than women twice my age have seen, but I'm a stronger person for it, change doesn't have to be a bad thing.

Molly MacArthur

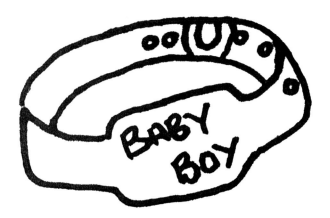

I was 16 when I found out I was pregnant. I had been with my boyfriend for 9 months and was living with him at his parents' home. I thought I would be delighted at being pregnant but I was so shocked when it actually happened that I was very scared and didn't know what to do. My boyfriend was desperate for me to keep the baby and after a few days of freaking out (not helped by constant morning sickness) I got used to the idea and realised it was what I wanted.

The pregnancy was all normal (very uncomfortable). Living with my partners parents wasn't working out as I didn't get on with them and really hated being there so we moved into my mum's house whilst searching for a place of our own. My partner was a self-employed window cleaner at the time.

I have had anxiety for the past 6 years causing me to be agoraphobic and nervous. It got bad while I was pregnant and I barely went out. When a family friend said they would rent us a 2 bed house we were over the moon to have somewhere secure to live as I was having arguments with my mum and it was causing a lot of stress. After we moved in my anxiety got worse as I didn't want to be left at home alone so I kept asking my partner to skip work. He began losing customers and we would argue a lot about it.

I went into labour 9 days overdue. The labour was 12 hours from start to finish. After planning to have a home birth I changed my mind 5 hours in. I had to push for 2 and a half hours before I finally gave birth to my 9lb 8oz baby boy called Camron. I remember the weight of him on my chest seconds after I experienced the worst pain. Luckily I only had a first degree tear but it was still extremely painful for weeks afterwards. I heard him screaming but couldn't look at him as the pain took over all of my senses. When I did see him I just felt shocked. I was glad when he was handed to his dad and passed around to my parents as I didn't feel comfortable holding him. He was born at 8pm so his dad had to leave at 11pm this terrified me that I was going to be left with the baby but now I am so glad it happened. I stayed up the whole night watching him and cuddling him and trying to get the hang of breast feeding (which hurt soo much). By the morning I was completely in love with my perfect little boy who was so strong and gorgeous.

We took him home the next day and settled into the routine quite easily. My boyfriend worked less and less as he wanted to be home with us. By the time Camron was about 9 months he had lost all of his customers and gave up work completely. This put a strain on the finances and the relationship between us. We argued more and more. We barely acted like we were in a relationship as the intimacy went after I had Camron. He still lives with me now 21 months later but we are not together. He just can't afford to move out.

Bringing up Camron was hard at times but mostly I loved it. My anxiety got extremely bad and this was the only downside to motherhood for me. I didn't take Camron out much and felt constantly guilty. I began going to a baby group when he was 10 months and met some other mums. The support helped hugely and I've gone every week since.

Having my son young has improved my life immensely as I am now battling my mental illness, and winning. I don't know where I would be without him. I do feel bad that I don't have lots of money or a great home for him to grow up in but I do have love, patience and energy by the bucket load for my special boy. He is beginning to speak now and it makes everything so worth it.

My advice for any young girls/ couples thinking about having a baby is this - wait till you have been together at least 2 years so that the intense love can pass and you can see if this is your lifelong partner (I was certain I had met my soul mate but now I know I was wrong). Also only get pregnant if you are 100% certain you want a baby and you are completely happy to put up with all of the millions of disadvantages of having a child, because trust me there are many e.g. mess, illness, tiredness etc.

I hope this letter helps/ inspires or just interests you :)

Eva.

I remember seeing his big brown eyes just watching me and how he just didn't cry. It was me doing the crying, I couldn't believe he was finally here after waiting such a long time and thinking he was stillborn when he came out silent; at that moment I had never been so grateful and I knew I was one lucky mommy to have such a strong little boy.

Yeah I'm a young mum but I wouldn't have it any other way and if I could go back in time I would do it all over again.

I was 17 when I found out I was pregnant and me and my partner had only been together for two months, a lot of people must have thought we were stupid. I was told we couldn't look after a baby, we couldn't afford our own house, we won't last together blah blah blah but we didn't listen because we knew we could. It wasn't like we didn't work, my partner was on a good wage with a great career and I was a trainee hairdresser just finishing college and working part time.

When I found out I told my boss we both agreed that I wouldn't be working there full time so we both decided I would work there till she found a new trainee. I then had no level 2 hairdressing course to go back to because they said I would be on my feet all the time so they didn't think it was a good idea me going onto level 2. Everyone thought I was basically just going to be a bum after that but I had a great family behind me (mine and my partners) and they knew different, they knew me.

"Preggers, #cough# SLUT!!" great, so just because I was young I was classed as a slut for having a bump under my top. College boys were as nasty as nasty could be and girls, well if looks could kill. I decided to do a childcare course at college and all the girls on the course were lovely and so excited about me having a baby but the rest around college were just horrible. Going into the food hall was like the walk of shame, but I knew that I wasn't any of the names they called me because everyone was wrong; we had our own little house in the middle of nowhere, we loved each other and most of all we loved our little boy.

Our pregnancy wasn't the best, scan after scan after scan every other week. The doctors said he might have to be born when he was just 27 weeks so I was prepared by having a steroid injection to help our boy's lungs develop but we were lucky he was fine and stayed put in there. At 36 weeks they tried to give me a sweep to encourage him before inducing me due to high blood pressure but he didn't budge and my blood pressure went down so I was left alone.

42 weeks + 1 day and 5 sweeps later he was here after an emergency section and swallowing his own poop and in intensive care for 3 days. He has taught me to never take anything for granted; I have never loved anyone or anything more than I love him.

For everyone who said we couldn't do it you were wrong. I'm proud of being a young mum and so what if I don't get to party like most people my age I'd rather stay in and have cuddles with my little man whilst watching Mickey Mouse's clubhouse on repeat.

Sophie

Gwen & Amy

I was living in a privately rented house with my young daughter and things were going ok until one day after really bad weather, my ceilings caved in! The house was condemned and I was forced to go and live in a hostel with Amy for four months as I had nowhere else to go. It was awful, I spent the first month sleeping on an air bed with my daughter. We had just one room with very little furniture in it. I had a cupboard and freezer in the shared kitchen but my food was constantly being stolen, I even had social care contacting me to say I wasn't providing food for my daughter! I didn't really make any friends, I didn't know who to trust. I felt useless and inadequate, I felt that I couldn't properly provide for my daughter. I visited the council almost daily, trying to get out of the hostel. I was also declined a community care grant seven times, even though I had lost most of my belongings. It has been a real struggle.

Hannah, Tom & PJ

When we moved into our housing association apartment, we thought we were really lucky, it was brand new and seemed perfect for our family to live in. After being there for nearly a year, we started noticing patches of mould appearing on walls, carpets and even our furniture. Our son PJ kept getting poorly and we knew there was something not quite right.

We reported the problems but didn't get anywhere as no one came out to see us. We then put in a complaint as the environment we were living in was really affecting our son and getting us down a lot. An environmental health officer finally visited us and took lots of photos, he said we shouldn't be living there until the problems were fixed. He contacted the housing association and told them it wasn't fit to live in and that we should be moved into alternative accommodation…. This didn't happen and we ended up only being able to use our living room with 2 big dehumidifiers in there also whilst the bedroom floors were taken up and re-done. They discovered there was very little insulation and that was why we were suffering from damp but they didn't correct it!

PJ still gets poorly and we are dreading the winter as it was last winter when all of the problems started. We are on the housing list to move but we are not getting anywhere with it, we feel trapped in the apartment and worry about all of us getting ill if the mould starts to re appear.

Kaci & Viola

When my little girl was born, she didn't look 'normal'. She had these huge eyes, long forehead, strange smile….. We thought she had Downs Syndrome. She had all the checks and tests and they came back that she was a perfect baby.

The hardest part was after…. People asked me if she had Downs Syndrome. It was very upsetting and got me down for quite a few months. She has now grown into her features and it's not noticeable. I love her very much and it wouldn't have mattered if she did have something wrong with her. I wouldn't change her for the world

Rhiannon, Kairon & Corey

When I was 17 years old I had my first son. He was planned but I didn't realise how much hard work it would be to be a mum. I was in and out of hospital throughout my pregnancy with liver problems and Pre Eclampsia.

The father of my son was with us physically but I felt that he wasn't there emotionally as I was getting no support from him. One year and sixteen days later, I gave birth to my second son, again I found it very hard as I was on my own, this time with both boys. Even though I find being a mum hard to cope with at times, I couldn't imagine life any other way.

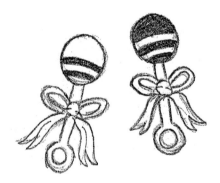

How It Feels Being A Parent…..

Being a parent is very complicated if you're me!

Firstly:-

I have a beautiful daughter(1 for later reference) with a woman who, at the time, I thought was the love of my life and was so happy when she was born.

However things change. The fact that she turned out to be an evil bitch and wouldn't let me stay over to do the night feeds and wouldn't let me do a thing for her or my daughter got on my wick.

To start with I was allowed to see her (my daughter) three times a week, Tuesday, Thursday and one day at the weekend, generally Sunday, but then the visits went down to Wednesday & Sunday.

Obviously this was extremely hard as I wanted to see her everyday possible, but her mum said NO!

After a while, I finally plucked up the courage to go to a solicitor to ask advice and legal proceedings started, however, the mother of my daughter managed to get round this somehow and my solicitor agreed to Wednesday & Sunday on my behalf. (Although they knew that I wanted more)

She then turned round to my solicitor and said that if I paid for my daughter, I could see her whenever, to which I replied "I am NOT having a pay-as-you-go-daughter as this would lower her to the grade of a mobile phone"

I was then advised by MY solicitor that this was the best option, as if I took her to court I would lose. Crap solicitor!

So I unwillingly agreed to this and things have been amicable for three years now until recently. She has now decided to get the CSA involved which is something that we BOTH agreed would NEVER happen.

During the time above, I met a girl who (without blowing my own trumpet) seemed to fall for me straight away. She was pregnant at the time (unbeknown to me).

I was running a pub at the time and she had asked me for a job, it had gone!

However, after a few weeks of coming into the pub, I finally asked her for her number, she then asked me for my fags, which I found bizarre, but never-the-less she wrote her number in my fag packet. I have to admit, I can't quite remember which night it was.

A few days later we had a quiz night at the pub, which she attended with her friend without her parents knowing, and throughout the evening, I was giving her some of the answers to the quiz and, although she was meant to be at home with her niece, she ended up staying the night!

Now, the thing for me, and her, was that it was a casual stay-over and nothing more but sex would come of it. Wrong!

Nearly three years later and we're still together!

In that time there have obviously been ups and downs.

I think the main down is the fact that at the time we got together, I still thought the sun shone out of my ex's arse and she could do no wrong. Also the fact that my ex had led me up the garden path by saying that if I sorted myself out there would be a chance of us getting back together (I didn't know she was evil at this time~!!!)

But as time went on I realised that there was NO chance of us getting back together and making a go of things and the girl in question sort of saved me!!!

We ended up getting together and she told me she was pregnant.

As you can imagine, I was initially shocked and horrified by this, but she then told me that the child was from previous relationship.

Obviously, at the time, I thought f**k me! What a s**g! How wrong could I have been?

I was still stunned when I said to her "That's fine we'll get through this". Maybe I didn't realise the responsibilities of taking on someone else's child, I just don't know. (2 for later reference)

What I do know, is that bit the BEST decision I have ever made!

The child in question is the brightest two and a half year old I have ever met. She is fantastically funny with pretty much everything she does and, most of all she is MINE.

At some point throughout her life, I will explain things to her, however, now is definitely not the right time.

But my ex seems to think so. She is forever tell my eldest that (2) is her step sister, if/when we get married, even though I and my current partner bring them up as sisters.

Now I know that she also has a right to know, but when she's three and a half, it's not the right time.

She WILL be told when she is old enough to understand.

During (2)'s lifetime, I gradually realised that (my partner (4)) became stressed under pressure.

This has been the main contributor to arguments, apart from money, within our relationship.

We have now been officially together for nearly three years and, on the whole, it has been fantastic.

However, there have been times where I felt like throttling her (4).

The thing that I find, is that staying calm is key. And this is something I have tried to instill in (4).

Generally, I AM the calm, collected parent, but recently, I have become more and more like (4). Stressed.

This is not a good thing for a number of reasons, obviously there are the two children involved, but also, there is a new addition to the family who is yet another girl aged five months.

She obviously picks up on the vibes around her, and this can be seen in everyday life.

If (1) or (2) cries, she cries.

Therefore I, and (4), probably need to be a lot calmer with the children.

However, this is extremely difficult when (1) comes to visit.

Obviously, I love her to bits, but she really is her mother's daughter. She can be evil when she wants to be.

The crux of it is:

If you are about to become/want to be a parent, enjoy the moments while you can, because they soon fade away and you have a mini-you running around. Which is the scariest thing ever.

Although, scarier than that, is mini ex's running around, now that REALLY IS scary.

The day my Life changed for the better

I couldn't believe my eyes my gorgeous princess was finally here after 9 long months of waiting I finally got to meet her.

I'd not long turned 18 and was out partying most weekends with my best friend at the time Lucy, we went out to what at the time was our local pub on a Friday night as they did karaoke which is where I met my daughter's biological father. I plucked up the courage to go and talk to him and we got chatting and started dating. Not long after I found out I was pregnant, I didn't know what to do or say I was so scared. I remember going for a walk down the canal and ringing my godmother who lives in Portsmouth and asking her for advice, later on that week I travelled down so we could sort things out and I could get my head around everything and think about what I was going to do. Before I left I told my partner at the time I was pregnant and he was over the moon but I told him I had to go away for a few days to get my head together, he was fine with this and we left each other on good terms, well that's what I thought.

When I was in Portsmouth I went through the usual procedure went doctors etc. I also kept my partner up to date, after a few days of me being away I found out my partner was cheating on me which I had already suspected at the time so I ended it which meant I had even more to think about such as if I could cope with being a single parent. The next big thing was having to tell my dad. Let's just say he wasn't pleased at all and I knew I had let him down big time. As the week went on I had come to my decision I decided it wasn't the right time for me to have a baby so we arranged an abortion back home in Leicester and up until the day before I was due to have the abortion I was definitely going ahead with it and then my conscience kicked in and I couldn't do it. I rang the clinic to cancel and it was the best decision I made.

As the months went on I kept in contact with my baby's father (I was doing all the informing, nothing from his end) I had agreed he could see her twice a week and maybe have her stay over once a week and he was fine with that, but as you can imagine nearing my due date I was getting fed up with him not asking me anything so we had a fall out, I didn't hear from him until somebody informed him I'd had my daughter and all I got was "how's you and baby" he hasn't seen her once since she was born and she's two and a half now.

During my pregnancy I knew I needed to think about mine and my baby's future so I knew I had to try and get a job so I popped in to my local pub where I had worked for about two-three years previously and asked the new manager for a job. Unfortunately somebody beat me to it. I went into the pub on a regular basis with my parents and one night (Monday) I was playing pool with the manager and we was having a bit of a flirt and a laugh and I remember asking him for some paper and a pen and I wrote my number down and hid it in his fag packet from that night we started texting.

The day after I had given him my number there was a quiz on at the pub which I attended with my friend, he asked me to stay the night and I did. From that day we would text and I would sleep over but this was only on a casual basis as he was still hooked on his ex partner and I knew he always wanted her back but I was falling for him and I couldn't stay away even though I knew it was wrong. After a few weeks I decided I had to tell him I was pregnant he was shocked and I quickly had to reassure him that it wasn't his and it was from a previous relationship, we carried on seeing each other through my whole pregnancy but he always said he didn't want anything to do with my baby and I understood.

Some people would call me stupid for sticking around but I was in love.

It was early hours of Boxing Day morning and I woke up in horrid pain. I think it was about 6am and that night I had stayed at my partner's house I text my mum as she was my birthing partner and said I think I'm in labour, I lasted until 12 o 'clock Boxing Day until I went to hospital. Before I left my partner said if you need me text me. On arrival at the hospital I was only 3cm dilated but it was awful pain and I text my partner to ask him to come down not thinking he would but he did and he stayed with me and my mum until the end he saw my little girl born and even had a tear in his eye. I remember vaguely as I was out of it due to having an epidural my dad walking in saying well done and he was proud of me but then he took my partner out to wet my daughter's head bearing in mind it was about 11pm Boxing night but I was so happy with my little princess I didn't care I had my mum.

They got back to the hospital at 2am and my partner told me he was proud and glad he came to the birth even though he got some stick off his ex partner (not that it had anything to do with her) but I didn't expect to see him again as he told me he wanted nothing to do with her.

My first night was awful I had no clue on what to do and my daughter wouldn't settle. I remember just getting her to sleep on me and the nurse came in and said try not to fall sleep with her on you, I wasn't impressed as you can imagine I'd had no sleep, but an hour or two later I got a text from my partner saying he wasn't allowed to see his eldest daughter as he had been at the hospital with me (petty I know) and he asked if he could come and see us. I obviously said yes and I was smiling like a Cheshire cat. As of that day we have been together and he has raised my little girl as his own.

Her biological dad has nothing to do with her and when the time is right we will sit her down and tell her everything but at this point in time she is far too little to understand. Since she was born two and a half years ago we have moved in to my partners house and he has proposed to me. We are due to get married in 2014. Yes it's been a rollercoaster, we have had our arguments as all couples do and I'll admit most of the time it's my fault as I worry about money and so on but now he has a steady job and hopefully things will start to get better.

We both had to adjust to everything as he had a daughter from a previous relationship and I had my daughter plus I had to get used to not living with my parents, that was very hard but I have adjusted and we have both taken on children. Of course my partners daughter doesn't call me mummy and I would never take that role away from her mum, she visits once a week and we all get along really well. I feel very privileged to be a part of her life, she's a very bright young girl and most of the time her and my daughter get along which is always good.

We now have a new addition to our family. She is now 5 months old and gorgeous, we feel very lucky to have 3 beautiful clever little girls and if I could go back and do it again I would.

I admit I had a few remarks come from my partner's friend when I was pregnant with my first child. I got told how hard it was and he would always get in my head saying things like "you sure you will cope, he will get back with his ex" and so on and I also got looked down on by my dad's cousin, she was always better than us well she thought she was and she would always look down her nose at me.

I was the bad one of the family, got knocked up at 18 but hey I don't care what anybody thinks - I'm in my own happy bubble with my wonderful family and I can't wait to see what the future throws at us as I know we can get through anything.

Dear Younger Me

As you have your Maternity photo-shoot you look down at your bump, fall completely in love and realise how big it actually is….. It's huge and looking like it's about to burst. You are getting so fed up, 2 weeks overdue! But you are loving every minute of it and you never complain.

It hasn't been an easy pregnancy. The morning sickness is terrible (Keep eating those Rich Tea biscuits in the morning!) The backache isn't very nice, the waddling is making people stare and the snide comments being made just because you are young can be upsetting. But it is so worth it and when you hold your baby all will be forgotten. It is a very big surprise being just 16 years old and finding out you are going to have a baby. But you are a brave girl and you take it in your stride. Your mum is an absolute angel and stands by you every step of the way, you learn a lot from her and you pray your baby loves you as much as you love her.

On September 11th 2011 you give birth to your beautiful baby girl Brooke. As she gets passed to you and you look into her eyes you smile because she is so perfect. That's the day your life changes. She is so tiny, weighing only 6lb 12 and she is the most amazing little gift in the world. You bond immediately and caring for her comes naturally to you so please stop worrying about how to be a great mum because truth be told, no-one actually knows!

For the first week of bringing her home all you do is watch her sleep and hold her. Her tiny little fingers and her tiny nose are what you have made and it feels incredible. Without fail every single morning your mum will ask how Brooke has slept, make you breakfast and hold her while you have a bath. You feel like the luckiest girl in the world. You sit and think to yourself 'This little girl is my world, my best friend and I will protect her for eternity'.

When Brooke is just 4 weeks old you enter into a 'Baby of the Year' competition. And she wins. You are so proud of her. Every single day she changes and becomes more and more amazing. Her first smile and giggle make you realise that she is your biggest achievement in life. People give you a lot of grief for being a 'young mum' but guess what… you prove them all wrong. You're just as good as anyone else no matter what age they are.

No-one said it would be easy and it certainly isn't…. the only perfume you have is baby sick, you constantly have it all down your shirt, you never have time to do your hair or make up and you always look rushed off your feet but when she smiles at you nothing seems to matter. Keep going, you're doing a great job.

Oh and don't feel bad about spending time with your friends on a Saturday night if you want to. Everyone needs a break and it doesn't make you a bad person just because you have a child now. If you didn't have a break once in a while you would go insane! So it is good for you and don't let anyone tell you different. Being a young mum isn't the worst thing in the world, it only means you get to meet your baby sooner, love her for longer and spend more precious time with her. With your love she will grow up to be a perfect little girl. What's wrong with that?

When Brooke is 2 months old you join a Progress group at a Sure Start Centre and it helps your confidence a lot! So keep going and working hard because towards the end you receive your certificate and a diploma. You watch your little girl grow up to be so beautiful and you make decisions for yours and her future to make it better.

In July 2012 you get accepted for College and what you want to do with your life becomes clear and things get better and better. At that moment you realise that you would do absolutely anything for this little girl to give her the best life she needs. It does only get better because after being accepted on the course you wanted to do, you and Brooke move into your first house together and you make it a beautiful home. Be proud of yourself because you have been so strong and no matter what bad things have been thrown at you, you kept your head held high. And so you should!

PS Don't let those jealous people get you down. No matter what bad things they say about you, it doesn't matter! You have it all and they are just not worth your time. One day they will realise just how hard being a parent is. No-one has the right to judge you unless they have walked a mile in your shoes. So let them hate and keep that head of yours held high!

There are times you feel so tired you wonder how you could possibly find the strength to carry on, but then she smiles at you. That cheesy little grin…. And you realise you can do it. Keep going.

Jazmine

Aged 17 when Brooke arrived.

I was 14 when I found out I was pregnant at the end of May 2010. My 15th birthday was August 30th and I was still in school. I'd been bullied majorly since I'd moved to the area 7 years back and when I found out I was pregnant I was the happiest girl alive!

Although it wasn't the ideal situation as I was in a majorly abusive relationship (violently and sexually) I was happy for once, I would have someone to give my love to, someone who would give their love back! I felt good, I knew it would be hard but I was going to do it! I stuck with his father as I was too scared to leave him, he was happy too (I think, he had lots of problems and things such as emotional issues and anger issues). I knew he wasn't all too happy when he continuously raped me and beat me bearing in mind I was pregnant!

I've been through a lot these last few years and not many people know as I've clammed up! But I continued to do well through my pregnancy. I had to leave school in the November as I had a chest infection and was bedbound for a week. I got a phone call telling me not to bother coming back until I'd given birth. I had to go to a pupil referral unit in the end for a little while and then I finally gave birth to my beautiful son Harry on 25th February 2011. He was perfect. All 10lb 6oz of him! He was 2 weeks early and I had to have a C-section because he was huge and breach! It wasn't easy as I couldn't move for a few days and I was too drugged up to do much! But I managed and then I went back to school 2 weeks later because I knew I had to get some qualifications! I managed to get 9 GCSEs, and they were not bad considering what I had been through!

My son is my life and the best thing that ever happened to me.

My journey started in 2010. I was 18 in my second year at college on a Health and Social Care course and me and my boyfriend had been together for 3 years. We hadn't been using any contraception for around a year as the thing we most longed for was a child. After unsuccessfully trying to conceive I was convinced something was wrong and we both went to the doctors for tests. Everything came back fine on Ben's half but I had been diagnosed by polycystic ovaries. I was heartbroken and convinced I would never be a mummy, the one thing I wanted more than anything else. I tried to put the idea to the back of my head and carry on but it's all I thought about. We carried on trying with no luck and I got my level 3 qualification and was applying for university to do a midwifery course.

Then in March I got some bad news. My great grandma, who our whole family was very close to, was very ill. She's had leukaemia for as long as I can remember and was fighting fit but she had now got pneumonia. It was March the 11th and something told me to take a pregnancy test. As I did I was waiting anxiously on my own, scared of looking at the result as I didn't want the heartbreak of a negative test again, but positive?? It couldn't be, the test must be wrong. I put it to the back of my mind and prepared for the 12 hour journey to Dundee to be with my great nan.

When me and my nan arrived at 3 o'clock at the hospital it was very clear she was in a bad way and just an hour and 25 minutes after we got there she passed away. After staying with her for an hour we went back to the hotel and I did 3 more tests. All positive? It couldn't be? Sure enough I went to the doctors and they confirmed it. I felt like my baby was a gift from my great nana. I gave birth on the 6th November 2011 after an hour and a half of pushing and into the world came the most perfect beautiful little boy I had ever seen.

My journey to get to where I am now has been a hard one and parenthood continues to have its difficulties, everyone thought I was too young to have a child but a massive gap in my heart has now been filled and I feel I am doing just fine, lovely boyfriend who works hard for us, a lovely house and a beautiful, cheeky son. He's now 9 months and on the move. He's into everything and teething like mad, sleepless nights for me and a baby stuck to my hip, but I wouldn't change it for a million years…. If having a child is what you want, go for it as it doesn't matter what other people think, being a mummy is the most challenging but rewarding thing ever.

Hayley

Toni,

I have a one year old daughter. I was 16. Still at school when I found out I was pregnant, turned out I was 16 weeks gone already! My mam went and told the school, all the teachers had their own opinion of how stupid I was and how I wouldn't cope!

Well my daughter's dad left the day she was born so I've done everything myself with my family's help. I got such horrible looks and comments off people when we were out shopping. Eventually I was sick of the names I actually stuck up for myself to one woman!

I still get comments now when I'm out and about with my daughter, who I am still breastfeeding! I managed to get 5 C's in my GCSEs even though I was 8 months gone and in agony, it's all rewarding knowing that my daughter has learnt everything from me and my family and I'm proud I'm a young mam!

xxxxx

Seventeen years old, sitting in my bedroom looking at a pregnancy test. The test was given as a freebie from some sort of teen sexual health organisation, so there are no instructions, no nothing. I hadn't even considered taking it, as of course there was no way that I could be pregnant. The stick is showing me two lines. I'm pretty sure that that means I'm pregnant, but can't be certain; like I said – no instructions. But I must have it wrong; it must be one line that means positive and two that means negative. I phone my best friend, to check. I don't really want to, but this is before the days that Smartphones are as popular as television sets and I don't have good old Google to hand. Riiiiing riiiiing! Riiiiing riiiiing! "Your call has been forwarded to the T-Mobile voicemail for..." Damn. By now I'm panicking. There's only one other friend who may know for sure, and we hadn't spoken properly for a while. She was a good friend though, right? I could ask her in confidence. So I did, and she said: "Sorayah, you're pregnant love."

And that was that. I was pregnant. I didn't cry, didn't laugh, didn't even react for a moment. I just said "Okay, thanks..." and hung up. I phoned my boyfriend. His reaction was the exact same as mine. "Er, oh. Er, okay... Um... I'll be round in a minute." I could hear all his friends laughing and joking in the background, as normal teenagers do. Whilst him and I sat on the phone realising we were about to have to become adults. Like, real, proper, actual adults.

My first worry was finishing my A-levels, going to uni. I had been doing well at sixth form; I was receiving my grades for my AS-levels soon and was expecting them to be good. I was expecting to go to a decent uni, study English Language and Literature and become a genius of some sort (okay, slight exaggeration, but you catch my drift). Right now was July. The summer holidays. The time to let down your hair and be free. I had no idea how far gone I was, but it was pretty obvious that some time during my second year of sixth form I would be pushing out a baby. And then, even if I did somehow manage to squeeze in my A-levels, I wouldn't be able to go to uni with a baby! For one, I'm sure we don't have 'family units' at university campuses here in the UK like they do in the US, and I had never even considered going to one of the local universities. And, let's say I did go to one of the local unis, how on Earth would I find the balance between writing my theories on post-1940 literature and flying aeroplanes of mashed up banana into the toothless landing point?

And then there were the worries of telling my family, of losing my youth, and, of course, actually being a mum. Could I really look after a child? My room looked like a World War II bomb scene, and I was going to have a baby living in it too? (To be fair, to this day my room still looks like a World War II bomb scene. That aspect of my life was unchanged by motherhood.) I also have a chronic illness called Crohn's disease (you may have heard of it. If you haven't, don't Google it, it's gross). While when I'm well I'm perfectly fine, there are times when I literally can't get out of bed for all the pain I'm in, and the lack of energy I have, and sometimes that can last for months. How could I look after a baby during those periods?

Anyway, let me move on a bit. After going to the doctors, I found out that I was three months pregnant. How had I managed to miss an entire trimester without even noticing? I hadn't had periods, so really there was no excuse. I guess it was a mixture of having irregular periods anyway, and being completely and utterly in denial. No excuse really though. I decided that I wanted to take a year out of sixth form and carry on with my A2-levels after that, but found out that I couldn't. The spec was changing, so my AS-level wouldn't fit with the following year's A2s. This was a hard blow. I really did not feel like I would be able to balance exams, being ill, and a baby all at once. When September came, I stopped going to sixth form altogether; my head was in a mess. Eventually I plucked up the courage to go and talk to my tutor and explain to her what was going on. And thank goodness I did. She convinced me to stay on at sixth form. She made it sound so easy; "You carry on coming in until you feel like you can't anymore, and then we'll send your work home to you. You'll be fine." She even made going to uni with a young child sound like it was so possible. So I continued going to sixth form throughout pregnancy, gave birth in February, worked on my coursework at home for a few weeks, then went back in two days a week, working at home the rest. My boyfriend and I had worked out a system where he could go to work and do his studies some days, while I did mine the others. It was hard, but it worked out. We also stayed living with my mum. There was no reason not to, as my daughter could have her own room when she got a bit bigger and we could save a hell of a lot of money that way too.

I finished my A-levels, I didn't do as well as I had hoped, but still good considering I had had a baby half way through the year with B-C grades. I then took a gap year before starting uni, as I wasn't ready to send the little one to nursery being so tiny.

That gap year was pretty hard. Things weren't great at home and my relationship with my mum was falling apart. The best thing at the time seemed to be to move into a place of our own. That was quite possibly the worst thing. For one, it was expensive. To say money was tight would be an understatement. And the worst thing was, we moved into quite an inconvenient place. Living in London, I can hardly call it 'the countryside', but it was right on the outskirts and there was no Underground station anywhere nearby. That, to any Londoner, might as well be the countryside. I didn't have many friends come to visit me, and I didn't often visit them either. I didn't know anyone nearby, and felt uncomfortable going to the baby groups because I was so much younger than the other mums there. No one seemed to talk to me. My boyfriend worked nights so would sleep in the day, so the majority of the time it was just me and my daughter alone. I became really lonely and depressed.

As soon as I started uni the following October, things changed. My daughter was at nursery, socialising with other kids, and I was able to socialise with other people my own age. Not only that, but it felt good to be doing something for myself. Even though I hadn't chosen to study English Language and Literature like I had always wanted, I chose a subject that I felt I would be able to balance with motherhood easier, and it was still based around language and literature so it didn't matter.

We moved back in to mums before I started my second year at uni for money saving reasons, and now things are much better. I'm closer to family and friends, and there are actually tube stations nearby. I'm home!

Now, my little miss is three, I'll be finishing university in May, and we're all happy. I've applied for a PGCE in secondary English, so hopefully this time next year I'll be an almost-qualified teacher. Things are going well. Life doesn't stop when you have a baby, your path just changes. For me, it's changed for the better.

Dear Abby

You don't realise this yet but you have a wonderful life ahead of you with so many opportunities. You are from a wealthy family (you don't know this either because you think that everyone lives in a big house) and you are actually a lot more intelligent than you think. If someone told you that one day you would gain both an honours degree and a Masters degree, you'd probably think they were nuts and then you'd reapply your make-up, hitch your skirt up and continue to bat your eyes at any male with a pulse.

Going out with a man twice your age is not clever and it will not make you popular. Your humour, good nature and genuine smile will do far more for you throughout your whole life than running away from home every night to have sex. And you're underage anyway! Going with a man that old isn't going to make your dad love you like you want him to. Your dad will always put your stepmother first; even after she loses her fight with cancer.

Let's talk about sex… you will get pregnant if you don't use contraception! Fact! I know you enjoy it (many girls your age don't) but think what getting pregnant now will do to your life chances. Ok, so you moved on from the older guy and found someone your own age; you will be friends with this man for the rest of your life, although you won't stay married to him like you think you will.

Having a baby now means that your life will be one constant struggle financially. No new clothes or shoes for you, young lady! It also means that you will be out of kilter with your friends. This will eventually even out but not until you are in your mid-forties!! Mid-forties? That's too old to even imagine right now! This is how it will go:

Age	What your friends will be doing	What you will be doing
Young Teen	Experimenting with alcohol; having a laugh; gaining qualifications.	Rubbing cream into your stomach to avoid stretch marks; squeezing into your jeans until even the safety pins won't hold; staying in watching telly to save up for the baby.
Older Teen	Going to university or earning money; meeting new people; concerts, pubs, clubs and parties; enjoying their freedom; experimenting with relationships.	Changing nappies; getting up in the middle of the night to a baby with colic; spending a lot of time on your own. Padlocking your pram outside the grocery store and taking the baby in with you because the area you live in is so rough.
Early 20s	Graduating; gaining employment; taking amazing sunny holidays abroad; buying beautiful clothes; dining out; falling in love; travelling the world.	Running around to get the children to school on time; holding down four part time jobs to keep up with the mortgage payments; studying at night school.

Age	What your friends will be doing	What you will be doing
Late 20s	Earning good money; still going on those amazing sunny holidays abroad (I'm so jealous); getting married; buying really nice houses.	Studying full time at university; dropping the kids off at the minders/ school or rushing to pick them up; trying to shop, cook, organise the kids' homework, parents' evenings, PTA meetings; struggling to pay the bills.
Early 30s	Having babies; still having those amazing sunny holidays abroad (how do they do that?); some working part time too which is probably how they afford the holidays!	Working hard at career; kids older now but a constant worry re: school grades, friendships and their emerging adolescence. Still unable to afford those holidays, meals out, etc.
Late 30s	Probably doing everything that I was doing in my early 20s but without the added pressure of study.	Finally... kids old enough so that I can go out. Friends all staying in with young children. Great!

Age	What your friends will be doing	What you will be doing
Early 40s	Probably doing everything that I was doing in my late 20s but without the added pressure of study (although some, strangely, choosing to retrain to accommodate family life).	Kids have flown the nest. Career going well; many friends still with children too young to leave. After a wait of over 20 years, I finally get to go on an amazing sunny holiday abroad…. it's amazing AND sunny!!
Late 40s	Holidays, meals, freedom; kids probably a worry to them but not preventing them from doing stuff.	Holidays, meals, freedom, kids grown.

Of course, having a baby is a wonderful thing and being a mother has given me so much pleasure too. But if I'd waited….???

I love that my daughter, nearing her 30s, has travelled the world extensively. I love that she has dived in exotic seas; climbed Mt Kilimanjaro; seen elephants, rhinos, hippos, giraffes, monkeys; picnicked amongst ancient ruins; eaten exotic food; camped under sunsets that look breathtakingly beautiful on the photos she has shown me. I love that she is a free spirit, yet responsible enough to hold down an amazing nursing career spanning over a decade now (one that she has practised in three different countries). She will have babies eventually, I hope, but in the meantime, she has a head and photo album full of places, people and experiences that I can only dream about; not to mention several tattoos she's picked up along the way: a bit of the old rebel in me ended up in her after all!

So, think twice Abby, you can have it ALL. All of it. Everything is waiting for you. Just think about the order you do it in.

Abby, age 46.

Being a young mum has taught me a lot about responsibility and budgeting money. I realise how hard being a mum is. Although I wish I had waited before I had a stable job and a good income before I started my family I wouldn't change anything about my son.

When I found out I was pregnant I expected it to be easy, I never expected to have pre-eclampsia and to be rushed for an emergency C section four weeks early. I wasn't prepared for anything especially for my baby to have a rare blood sugar disorder and giving me 2 different meds 3 times a day every day for four weeks we spent down the hospital with our poorly baby.

If I could give myself any advice looking back I would say relax more and always expect the unexpected and be prepared for anything.

The Future is looking Bright

I was horrified when I knew I was pregnant I was so young, my baby is eighteen months old and I am still at school.

My mum looked after my baby for a start then I realised it should be my responsibility. I learnt the hard way. I love being a mum it is the best job in the world although it is hard managing bringing up a child going to school and now managing my own tenancy.

I found the sleepless night, tantrums, not being able to go out when I wanted and not knowing why my baby was crying really difficult.

One of the hardest things is getting up early getting a baby ready then going to school. The coming home doing my homework while trying to look after my little boy

I need to stay at school to get my GCSE grades because I want to be a midwife. I want to be able to support my son I would like to be able to afford for him to go to a private school I do not want him to hang round on street corners causing trouble or taking drugs.

My baby boy cheers me up every day, I am proud of myself and how I have managed so far. I love it when he tells me he loves me and the future is looking brighter

Rebecca Price

Forget drugs – having a baby is the greatest high you'll ever feel. That perfect moment you hold the tiny person you've been protecting for all these months and you feel that little hand grasping your finger and you just know. All the backache and the mood swings and the ligaments stretching (not to mention the labour you went through) all become worth it. You stare into your baby's eyes and feel the most intense kind of warmth. A love that is unconditional and consuming, and don't get me wrong there are gonna be times when your child's driving you nuts and you need to have a break if just for a few hours but even in that time away it's like you're missing a limb.

For the 9 months and 15 and a half days my little man was in my tummy, I loved him, but the moment I saw him I fell in love. His little Yoda face and beautiful huge brown eyes, his thick black hair, his long hands, feet and legs – he was perfect.

In the times I feel broken he's what keeps me sane. He reminds me that though everything is going terribly wrong, he is my one good thing. He's my first smile in the morning, my favourite hugger and the single funniest being on Earth!

Jenson, I love you all the stars in the sky, the mass of the sun and to the moon and back.

PS If I have any advice (that for me has been a godsend) it's to remind yourself of what being a young parent means. It's not another way of saying "bad mum" or "irresponsible and untrustworthy" It just means you work that little bit harder, you're that little bit more determined and it'll take a little bit longer but when you finally get there it's sure as hell worth it!

Minnie, 19
Mother to Jenson

My Bump

My bump just appeared from nowhere, it never gave me a chance to think about it. It has gradually squeezed out my inny button to an outy. I feel guilty other mums feel good and are proud about their bumps. I am not so sure.

As my pregnancy has progressed I have grossed out on a daily basis it feels like bubbles moving around inside of me, popping on the inside of my tummy.

What is in there, an alien?

How much longer do I have to endure this thing stuck out in front of me? It gets in my way I can no longer squeeze through gaps and it is so heavy to carry around.

I cannot wait until it is gone. It will all be worth it the end when my bump is no longer stuck on the in front of me, but my beautiful baby who I can hold in my arms.

KF, Young Parent Loughborough Foyer
2010

Dear A Little Younger Amie,

So you're enjoying life, blissfully unaware that in little over 9 months time things change drastically. You have met the love of your life (yes, I know you're only 17) and are having the time of your life, being a teenager.

In August 2011 you will find out you're pregnant. Expecting a baby. Going to be a mum!

Please don't think that Mum and Dad will hate you because they won't, trust me. You finally pluck up to tell mum, thinking over and over in your head what their reactions might be. Yes, they will be shocked but you will be very surprised. I think most parents think they feel the need to ask 'well, what are you going to do?' You will have to tell Daniel's mum the 'good' news too, thankfully his dad will be fast asleep. With Daniel not taking anything seriously at the moment, he will laugh and you feel alone.

But being alone is not what you will be throughout the difficult 9 months ahead. The support you will receive from mum and dad, the 'in laws' and extended family will be extraordinary to say the least. Daniel will shock you most. You hear about teenage mums not having a father for their baby, not having someone their when you see the 'alien inside your tummy' for the first time on a tv screen.

Daniel is the very opposite. Missing lessons at college to come with you to see the midwife (it's not as bad as it sounds), holding your hand when you discover that your baby has a 'hamburger not a hotdog'. Yes! You are carrying a little girl, the girl you have longed for since you found out you was expecting.

The next 6 months fly by. Your daughter kicking you, dancing inside your growing bump. You will suffer from back ache and I mean suffer! Constant walks around the block will not help! The 19th March 2012 will come and go and off to the hospital you go for induction. Daniel is still there, don't worry, he is not leaving your side, even through the 'gory' bits. You make yourself a promise to not leave the hospital without your baby as you find out that your baby is not one to make a show.

After days lying in that bed, '"mooing" with pain, you hear the words that will shock you. Mum will have to go outside as she finds it hard. You need A EMERGENCY CAESEREAN SECTION! You're only 17, you're not old enough to cope with all of this. But you will and you do.

On the 3rd April 2012 at 3.06 you finally meet your gorgeous bundle of joy, naming her Lola Joy Charley Sim. Daniel's face fills with pride as he comes to terms with being a father.

8 months on and he is still coming to terms with this little girl rolling around, giggling at him. You sit back and watch.

Did I forget to mention, you're in your own house with your own family. You will have to grow up so fast. You're a mum now to Lola, nothing else matters in the world.

Here's some advice Amie:

- Look forward and never look back.

- Make use of the 'Under 19 mum and baby' groups as everyone there understands you. No older mums to look down on you.

- Don't wish your life away by planning the future. Take every day as it comes and love your daughter like you've never loved before. Remember, your love will only grow.

- Don't listen to 'advice' other mums give you. Do it your way. You're her mum, you know best!

All my love,

A little older,

AMIE

x

Dear Ivie-Emma

You were born on 6th December at 2.03am. It was a home birth, under the Christmas tree with the fire on.

I played Just Dance for 2 hours to keep active and help bring labour on, I had contractions all the next day and after a hot bath and a huge pie and chips dinner, my waters broke at 7pm on the 5th December. I was in established labour for just 3 hours.

Labour was so exciting, because I knew I would be meeting you really soon. After 9 months of keeping you in my tummy, feeling your kicks, wiggles and hiccups, I was desperate to see you.

Giving birth hurt way more than I thought was even possible, but the second I held you in my arms the pain went away.

It was the most amazing moment, it was like everything stopped. You were the tiniest, most perfect, beautiful thing I have ever seen.

Having a home birth was perfect, it was so relaxed. I had your Nanna and Grandad by my side, they were both there through the whole labour and got to watch you being born.

I really loved being pregnant, having a bump, getting to listen to your heartbeat, feeling all of your kicks and wiggles. As much as labour and giving birth hurt, I loved it and all the emotions that went with it.

But getting to hold you, watch you grow and learn new things, waking up to your beautiful face every morning and thinking of all the exciting things to come, really is the most perfect thing.

Lots and lots of love, kisses and cuddles,

Mummy xoxoxo

Georgina, 16

A Day in the Life of...

This section is a chance for us to get to know people and learn about what they do each day. This article is about Jade, a young mum at the project. She takes us through her daily routine and highlights the challenges that come with it.

At 7am I wake up and get Kieran out of his cot and put him in his bouncer. I put on cbeebies while I make my breakfast and get dressed for College. I then change Kieran's nappy and get him dressed for nursery. I have my bag and Kieran's ready the night before and put them on the pushchair. I then give Kieran his bottle and walk to get on the bus for College.

My favourite parts of the day would be giving Kieran his first cuddle when he wakes up and picking him up from nursery as I've missed him all day. Being a mum and going to College is challenging because it's hard to get my work done on time while he's awake. It's difficult being a mum because you don't get a minute to yourself, but it's enjoyable at the same time as you get to watch him develop.

Once I get home, he plays in his walker while I make his dinner. I then feed him his dinner and have mine. Then I give him a shower and get him ready for bed at 8pm. I then do the cleaning and go to bed ready for another day.

People often think they know full well the advantages and disadvantages of being a teen mum, with the advantages being that oh-so-glamorous and easy lifestyle of living on benefits, and the disadvantages being the general ruin of your whole entire life. However, for those more open minded people I thought I'd share with you the top 10 best and worst things about being a young mum.

Top 10 Best Things about being a young mum:

1. You can just about get away with sharing the same clothes as your child (if they are the same gender) without looking inappropriate.

2. You can still vaguely remember doing GCSE's - which actually helps a lot when they are doing theirs.

3. You have so much more energy before you reach 30. By that time you can (should) stop running round after them.

4. You're so poor when they are babies that your financial situation can only really get better.

5. You never really knew what it was like to have freedom, as in proper adult freedom, so you don't have it to miss.

6. Your skin is more stretchy in your youth so it is more likely to repair itself to a pre-pregnancy state.

7. At 34 you could sell up and leave the world of responsibility forever (without the 'what if' questions).

8. Your children's chums all add you as Facebook friends - great for getting an insight into their world (not so great if you'd rather not know - or you'd rather they didn't know yours).

9. Being constantly reminded of how young you are is actually quite nice in your thirties.

10. You have more chance of living to see your great, great, great grandchildren!

Top 10 Worst Things about being a young mum:

1. You never had a 'pre-pregnancy body' (or not for long enough to make the most of it anyway!).

2. For many young mums, the first time you fall in love will be the day you meet your child. No bloke can EVER compete with that.

3. The unplanned-ness of it all can mean that siblings have to wait - in my case my son will be waiting forever

4. Even though you love the bright colours and fizzy drink taste, unfortunately so will your child. Having Alcopops in the house are just not work the explaining...

5. It's disappointing when you think you're a cool young mum and then have to come to terms with the fact that your child is still embarassed to be seen out with you.

6. Savings. Or lack of. How exactly to people ever get them and not need to spend them???

7. Some experiences you just cannot relate to. 'Going to the gym' just seems like an expensive and pointless equivalent of pushing a buggy up a steep hill or playing football with a hyper five year old!

8. 'Going travelling to find yourself' doesn't mean anything to you (especially when going on holidays with children you seem to spend most of your time just trying to find places that have child-friendly menus). By the time the kids have left home and you can go travelling on your own, you'd pretty much hope that you know who you are by then.

9. You missed the chance to skip lectures and have a Duvet Day. Instead you were more likely to be skipping lectures because your child was ill, and then you can't wait to get back to Uni for a break!

10. An 'impromptu night out' is impossible in your tweens / twenties ('oh wait, I'll just sort out a babysitter, right - I can do three weeks on Saturday... hello?). When you reach your thirties and suddenly find yourself with unlimited free time - grinding drunkenly with randoms and flashing to the bouncers doesn't quite have the same appeal when you run a high risk of bumping into your child or their friends....

This article was originally published on telegraph.co.uk

Dear Charmaine,

When I found out I was pregnant I thought my life was over, I thought nobody would ever talk to me again, I thought it was the start of a life of pain and misery. But when I told mum, yeah I got a telling off but then couple of days later we found ourselves out shopping for Moses Baskets.

Throughout my whole pregnancy I didn't like it cause it was so surreal I was still going to school being with everyone who was my age but I felt so out of place, and so much more mature than them. But in some ways I liked it, having that closeness with my baby was perfect. My brother Lewis who is also my best friend said "look Charm you will always have a best friend, you will never be lonely ever again" since then I changed, I knew he was so right and I couldn't wait till I had my baby in my arms.

The birth was almost as long as the pregnancy in and out of hospital up and down stairs trying to get him out pushing for over 2 hours and in the end with the help of forceps and 40 hours of me screaming Eli was here. I was scared and could only take one day at a time. If I looked too far into the future I would scare myself and start crying.

But now I am looking forward to our beautiful future just me and Eli taking on the world. We have each other to take care of always and forever. I'm starting college to become a hairdresser and starting driving lessons soon so things are really starting to look up for us right now. We are both so happy right now.

If I could have changed something it would have just been to have waited till I was older in a stable relationship with a house and job and car.

Dear 16 year old me,

Stop crying little lady, it's time to pull your socks up. This next year is going to be the most difficult but rewarding year of your life. Your life is going to change for the better thanks to that beautiful little boy so don't be scared, be grateful.

You're going to lose a lot of your friends but don't get upset by it - you'll eventually see that they never were or will be your proper friends. Jen and Joel will continue to be your rock. Appreciate them now, they will help you out millions. You'll realise your mum is your best friend, so when you get that cute little flat don't be worried, she'll be up everyday. Show her how much you love her everyday, she becomes the best nana you could imagine, and don't worry about the rest of the idiots you called friends, the girls at Sure Start become some of the best friends you could ever ask for. So when you get that offer to go to Sure Start, then go (it's not what you think I promise).

You're in for a rough ride, rougher than most but you'll be so much stronger by the end of it. Once little man is born things are hard in that hospital. The only thing I can say to help you out, is the intensive care trips don't last long and in 8 days you will both be fine and back at home, so don't panic!

There's so much I want to tell you but not much time, so here:
- your body won't be the same, save time and stop worrying about it
- when weaning Frankie, do not give him ginger or dairy (it will save lots of time and doctor's trips)
- take photos every day
- smile through it all.

Things with Scott will get difficult so stop arguing, it'll all be fine. He is a good man and amazing father. Cherish your friends and adore your mother is the best piece of advice I could give you because you will be a good mum, it's just a long hard journey there.

So be brave, keep smiling, because after this year it will start to look up. Make sure you tell your boy you love him everyday.

Good luck sweetie you're going to need it.

Lots of love

18 year old Paris xxx

A book like this would never be possible without the time, generosity and huge effort on the part of our wonderful letter writers, illustrators, the county Young Parents Forum and the support of Leicestershire's Teenage Pregnancy Partnership.

To all of the parents who took the time to put pen to paper, we would like to say a huge thank you! It is so inspiring that you were prepared to share your experiences, positive and not-so-positive, to highlight some of the challenges that young parents today can face; the incredible strength that it takes to be a parent, and the fact that once you have your little bundle (or bundles!) of joy you would walk to the ends of the earth and back to make sure they will have the best life that you could possibly provide for them.

Being a young parent can mean that you are likely to face difficult experiences and that your life will suddenly seem to become everyone's business. As you will see from the stories in this book there is a resounding message –keep your head held high! Things won't always be easy but you can do it and although it helps to have supportive people around you, you will find the strength from reserves that you didn't know existed to put your child at the forefront of your world.

A big thank you must go to our illustrators, Jess and Tina, who created the beautiful drawings we have used throughout the book.

An equally big thank you goes to the wonderful young women who volunteer as part of our Young Parents Forum. The forum gives young parents (to-be) the opportunity to have a voice around the support they would like to see in place for those who become parents under the age of 20. I hope you agree that the time and effort you have put in to make this book happen has been worth it.

And finally, a huge thank you goes to those involved in the Leicestershire Teenage Pregnancy Partnership, from the Implementation team, to the wider Partnership, to the Executive Board, all supported by the tireless hard work and energy of Katie Phillips.

In no particular order and for a range of different things including letters, support, practical help and inspiration, thank-you to:

Sarah, Jess, Kacie, Chris, Toni, Molly, Eva, Sophie, Gwen, Hannah, Tom, Kaci, Rhiannon, Kairon, Jazmine, Hayley, Toni, Abby, Soroyah, Rebecca, Minnie, Amie, Kim, Charmaine, Paris, Kate, Tina, Katie P, Toni B, Sara, Sam E, Vanessa, Thelma, Dawn, Leah, Joelle, Katie R, Donna, Jade, Jan and Stephen.

Vicki x

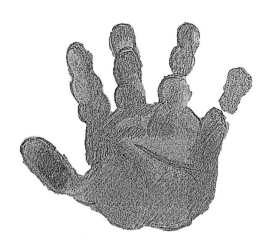

For every copy of this book sold, a donation will be given to the Bodie Hodges Foundation.

Bodie's mum Donna was instrumental in helping to set up our most successful learning programme for young parents (to-be) and supporting many young women to have improved self-confidence and self-belief.

The Babysteps programme has now been running for a number of years and Donna's enthusiasm, love and involvement has helped to shape its success. Thank you Donna x

More more information about the foundation, visit
www.facebook.com/BodieHodgesFoundation

Children are an amazing blessing and I hope that you have enjoyed reading the stories from other young parents. The love that we feel for our children is sometimes hard to put into words, there are days when things are tough and we may be finding life difficult, but a smile from a little person usually eases our struggles. The young parents that I have had the privilege to work with are full of love and determination for their children. The things they are now achieving did not seem possible until a little person came along and gave them the courage to do well. Our little boy is no longer with us but every day, with the help of his big sister, he gives us the courage to do good things in his memory.

The Bodie Hodges Foundation was set up in the summer of 2012 after Bodie died following a choking accident. Bodie was our baby boy and died at 10 months old. The hole that he has left in our family will never be filled by anyone or anything. Bodie spent two weeks in hospital in the hope that his brain would recover but sadly this was not the case. We wanted some good to come from such a tragic situation and so our brave and strong boy went on to be an Organ Donor. He has saved the lives of 4 children all under the age of 2, who would have died without Bodie's Liver, Bowel and heart valves. We are proud that Bodie could be an Organ Donor and want to encourage you to register yourself and your child on the Organ Donation register and tell your family about your wishes.
We promised Bodie when we were in hospital that we would do good things in his memory. At this point we weren't sure what those good things would be or how much support we would receive once we shared our ideas about the foundation.

We were given a holiday to Spain and Cornwall by some very generous friends. Going away without Bodie was really hard, we wanted to be a family of four not three. Despite the fact that our grief was so raw, there were moments during those holidays where we laughed, we felt relaxed and we began to rebuild. Our beautiful daughter Lyla, who we feel blessed to have every day, gives us a reason to carry on and to build Bodie's legacy. A holiday gave us time to support her and show her the love she needed. It was after these holidays that our vision for the Foundation started to take shape.

Our aim is to raise 150,000 to buy a holiday home for families in the East Midlands to use after the death of a child under the age of 18. We want to provide a place where they can spend some time as a family to also support siblings with their loss.

We would love you to follow us on Facebook or Twitter and get involved with our fundraising.

www.facebook.com/BodieHodgesFoundation
www.twitter.com/Bodie_Hodges